INVENTIONS NO ONE MENTIONS

by Chip Lovitt

SCHOLASTIC INC.
New York Toronto London Auckland Sydney

This book is dedicated to Lillian,
who provided invaluable research assistance.

The author wishes to thank Joe Oldham of *Popular Mechanics* magazine for his cooperation and Phyllis Braun for her encouragement.

The illustrations on the following pages are reprinted from *Popular Mechanics* © The Hearst Corporation. All Rights Reserved: pp. 5, 7, 9, 11, 13, 17, 23, 24, 25, 27, 29, 31, 33, 37, 45, 47, 49, 51, 52, 59, 63, 65, 66, 67, 69, 71, 75.

Illustrations on the following pages courtesy of U.S. Patent Office: pp. 8, 15, 19, 20, 35, 39, 41, 42, 55, 57, 61, 71 (bottom), 73.

Book Design by Ira Hechtlinger

ISBN 0-590-33209-0

12 11 10 9 8 7 6 5 4 3   0 1 2/9

Printed in the U.S.A.   28

First Scholastic printing, November 1987

Contents

"Necessity is the mother of invention."

— an old Latin saying

Some inventions — the light bulb, the telephone, the automobile — were important from the day they were created, and were destined to change our lives. Other inventions were destined for something else — the wastebasket! The real but ridiculous inventions in this book fall mostly into this second group — which may have been unfortunate for the inventors, but good for the public. No one really needed these inventions, and some of them would have created more harm than good.

An inventor didn't have to be a genius like Edison to get a patent from the United States Patent Office in Washington, DC. These inventors, of the late 19th and early 20th centuries, had only to provide a written description of their inventions, a drawing, and a miniature working model. In the early days of the Patent Office, examiners didn't really check out the claims of inventors or look into the safety aspects of their inventions.

It's been said that genius is 1% inspiration and 99% perspiration, meaning it takes a lot of work to sell a new idea. But in the case of these inventions, it was more like 1% inspiration and 99% imagination. As you'll soon see, some of these geniuses had wild imaginations.

The Silly Inventions Hall of Fame

You might think these oddball inventions are too ridiculous to be true. But believe it or not, they're for real. No matter what their intentions, these inventions do have a place in history — as the silliest, strangest, and funniest ever made!

Have Your Cup and Eat It, Too!

The Chocolate Cookie Cup

The inventor of this cracked cup idea proposed it as an alternative to serving cookies *and* milk. The cup was made out of graham cracker meal and coated with chocolate. You could drink the milk in the cup and then eat the cup. Of course, you had a problem if you wanted to eat the cookie first and then wash it down with milk. If you waited too long, the cup got soggy, which was one of the reasons it never caught on. Too bad, but that was the way the cookie crumbled.

An Air-Brained Scheme

The Flying Automobile

This was exactly what the name said. It was an actual car bolted to a single-engine propeller plane. It was meant for drivers in a hurry. If a driver was stuck in traffic, all he or she had to do was start the plane's engine and wait for the propeller to lift the car and plane into the air. It was tested in actual flight in the late 1940s. Its first flight brought the inventor's hopes back down to earth in a hurry. Somebody forgot to fill the fuel tank of the Flying Automobile, and it crashed and was destroyed. This idea never got off the ground again.

For Chewsy Folks

The Chewing Gum Locket

"Does your chewing gum lose its flavor on the bedpost overnight?" asked the lyrics of a 1960s song. Seventy years earlier, the same thought must have occurred to the inventor of this ultimate flavor saver. The Chewing Gum Locket looked just like an ordinary locket. But instead of concealing a picture of a sweetheart inside, it had another type of sweet — a piece of chewed chewing gum. The locket was airtight when closed, said the inventor, and it would keep the gum fresh and ready for a second chewing an hour — or even a day — later. Recycling materials may be fine, but storing ABC (already been chewed) gum in a locket was an idea choosy chewers found a bit hard to swallow.

A Bald-Faced Lie

The Hair-Growing Hat

This 1920s device looked suspiciously like spare parts from an electric lamp. Its creator promised: "It can grow a full head of hair even on a totally bald man." If this bald-faced lie sounded impossible, there was a good reason. It *was* impossible.

Baldness occurs because the hair roots are dead and not just asleep or dormant as the inventor believed.

A Merry-Go-Drowned

The Water Wheel

You might call this invention a merry-go-drowned. This funny ferris wheel dunked campers into the water, then lifted them out again. "It is a desirable addition to any camp," said the inventor in 1924. That may have been true as long as one of the camp's activities happened to be water torture. The wheel supposedly turned on water current alone. But if the current stopped, so did the wheel, leaving at least one unlucky camper underwater!

Hilarious Household Help

There was no place like home for inventors. Whether it was the kitchen, the playroom, or the cellar, there was always room for another new product. These household helpers may not lend themselves to use in your everyday life, but they've earned a place in your everyday laughs!

Dishes with Ap-peal

Peeling Plates

Hate doing dishes? Then these 1920s Peeling Plates were for you. Instead of washing the plates, you merely peeled off one of a dozen layers to reveal a clean surface below. There was no muss, no fuss, but most people thought this was an idea without any ap-peal at all!

What's Snooze?

The Improved Alarm Clock

There are light sleepers and heavy sleepers. Some heavy sleepers could sleep through an earthquake. Almost nothing will get them out of bed.

To remedy the situation, an inventor in 1882 created what he thought would be a failure-free alarm clock. It consisted of a wooden frame suspended over the sleeper's head and connected to a nearby alarm clock. At the right time, the alarm would release the wooden frame onto the head of the sleeper. The frame, said the inventor, would "strike a light blow, sufficient to awaken the sleeper, but not heavy enough to cause pain." This invention was not just a bomb, it was a time bomb and a total nightmare for sleepers. Mercifully, it dropped from sight before it dropped on too many heads.

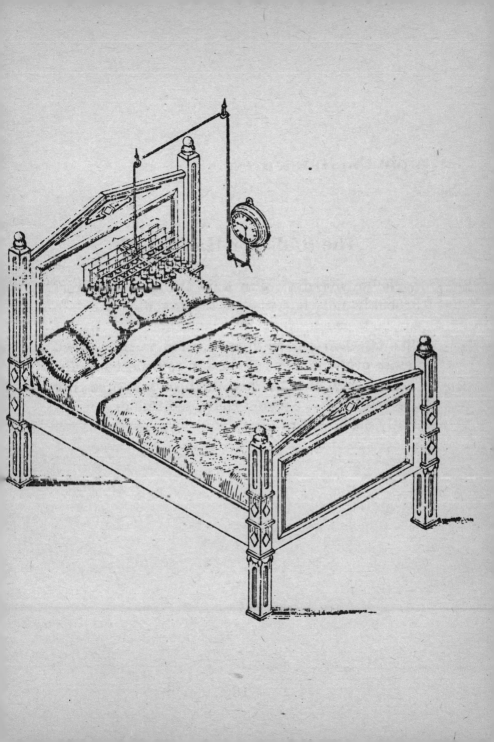

Join the Hair Farce

The Radiator Hair Dryer

Would you dry your hair using a radiator? Probably not, but one 1920s inventor tried to convince people that this was a hot idea. He set up a fan near a radiator and fitted a cone-shaped device over the front of the fan to collect hot air. The fan then blew the hot air through a tube onto the user's hair. Anyone could see this dryer was really not so hot at all.

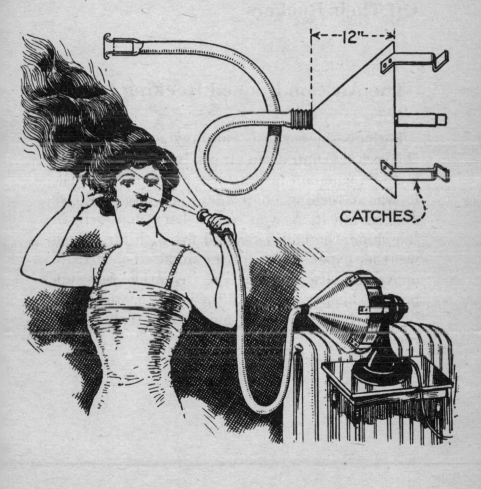

—12"—

CATCHES

Off Their Rockers

The Air-Conditioned Rocking Chair

Perhaps the earliest, and maybe the only, use of a rocking chair as an air conditioner dates back to 1869, when an inventor created this silly seat. It was a rocking chair that had large bellows underneath it. As you rocked back and forth in the chair, the bellows would fill with air, which was then expelled through the snake's-head fixture above the sitter's head. The invention was supposed to keep you cool, but the inventor was really full of wind, and many said he was truly off his rocker!

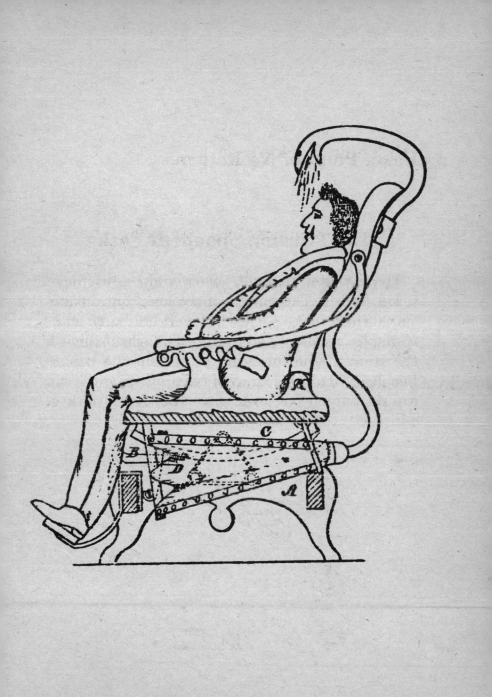

Pasta Point of No Return

The Twirling Spaghetti Fork

The inventor thought this would be his meal ticket for life. The handle of the fork contained a small wheel that a spaghetti lover could turn with a simple motion of the thumb. The wheel turned the tines of the fork and pulled up the pasta. People have always enjoyed twirling spaghetti on a fork, but no one ever gave this funny fork a whirl.

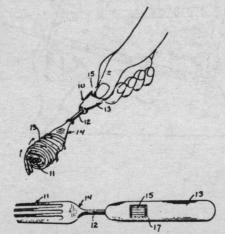

Kids' Stuff

Adults have always been trying to make children behave better. But when inventors got into the act, they came up with some remarkably strange remedies. Their inventions didn't last and kids, luckily, don't know what they missed.

A Solution for Slouching

The Chin Lifter

Designed for slouching students, the Chin Lifter was actually tested in schools more than seventy years ago. It featured a round metal cup that held up the chin, not too comfortably, and was supported by a rigid metal pole attached to the edge of the desk. The inventor said the device would keep the student the right distance from the desk and writing paper. But the Chin Lifter got failing marks from students who tried it. As far as they were concerned, the right distance any kid should be from this stupid school supply was about a million miles away!

Girl Writing with Chin
Lifter in Use

Not the Write Idea

The Pencil Clip

This invention fit on a student's finger like a ring. The ring had a little clip through which you could stick a pencil. Thus, according to the inventor, the pencil was always ready for writing and could never get stolen or lost. If you forgot about the Pencil Clip, however, and tried to scratch your head, you could lose something else — your eye. As a result, the Pencil Clip was written off in record time.

A Pain in the Neck

The Napkin Holder

It's not in fashion now to tuck a napkin under your chin when you eat. But in 1909, all tots and teens tucked their napkins under their chins. One inventor was determined to make sure kids didn't drop their napkins, so he designed an improved napkin holder. It was a metal band that fastened around the neck. On the front half of the band was another metal strip that lifted up so a napkin could be slipped in and held securely. Kids everywhere described this invention as simply a pain in the neck.

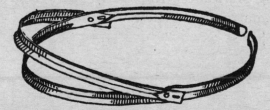

It's Snow Joke

The Mechanical Snowball Thrower

The Mechanical Snowball Thrower was (choose the best answer):

a) a failure made of wood.
b) a device that mechanically and automatically threw snowballs during snowball fights — once you had loaded them in.
c) a stupid idea.
d) all of the above.

The correct answer is *d*. Kids gave this flaky invention the cold shoulder. When it comes to throwing snowballs, kids have always preferred to take matters into their own hands.

Not So Bright Ideas

Inventors have always sought to use electricity in new ways. These inventions, however, have to be among the dimmest ideas in this field. In the end, all these not so bright ideas were taken quite lightly.

Bag It!

The Flashlight Purse

No one would have a hard time finding keys in a handbag if this invention had caught on. It was a regular purse with a small but powerful light built inside. The light was battery powered, and it went on as soon as the purse was unfastened. The inventor had some bigger ideas, too. He envisioned putting bigger lights into bigger purses and suitcases once the Flashlight Purse became a success. But this flashy fashion accessory faded into history.

Leaves Doctors in Stitches

Adjustable Surgeon's Lamp

You won't find any mention of this marvel in medical textbooks. The Adjustable Surgeon's Lamp was introduced in 1916, when many operations were done in dimly lit homes. It was meant to provide doctors with a source of bright light. A battery pack in the doctor's shirt pocket powered the lamp, which was held by biting down on a mouthpiece. By a simple movement of the head, a doctor could shine light wherever it was needed. This idea had doctors in stitches.

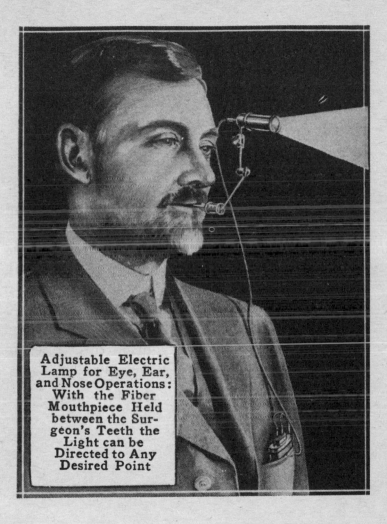

Adjustable Electric Lamp for Eye, Ear, and Nose Operations: With the Fiber Mouthpiece Held between the Surgeon's Teeth the Light can be Directed to Any Desired Point

A Shot in the Dark

The Flashlight Gun

Intended for policemen, this 1927 Flashlight Gun had two triggers. One fired real bullets. The other shot a beam of light from a device on top of the bullet barrel. It was hoped that the criminal, blinded by the light, would cower in fear and then surrender. But a police officer would be in big trouble if he needed some firepower and pulled the wrong trigger. This invention threatened to turn the police force into a police farce!

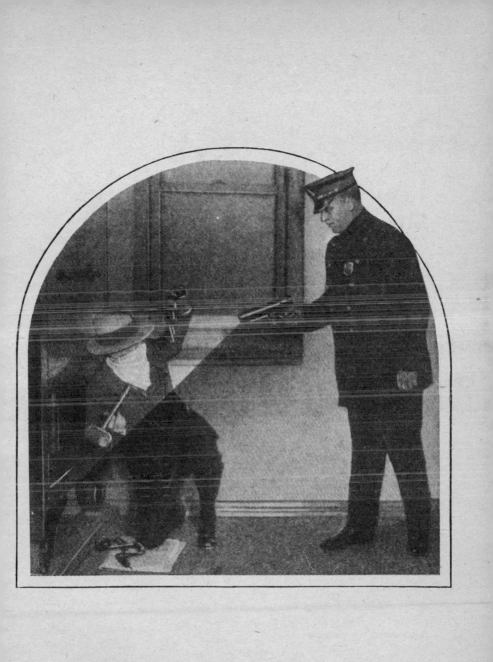

Lifesavers and Other
Great Escapes

"Safety first," could have been the motto of the inventors of these oddball items. In the face of fire or flood, these inventors were ready to come to the rescue with their creations. But would you trust your life to these loony lifesavers?

Registered to Float

An Improved Life Preserver

You wore this around your neck. It had a miniature pump and inflatable float to keep your head bobbing above the water. All you had to do to save yourself, said the inventor, was stay calm and use your head.

Wash Over Me While I Sleep

The Unsinkable Life Bed

If the *Titanic* had had these beds, all of the passengers might have been saved when the ill-fated luxury liner sank in 1912. Or so claimed the French inventor of this combination bed and life-boat. The bed would float high enough above the water to prevent even the heaviest passenger from sinking. It's shown here being demonstrated on the Seine River in Paris in 1915. The bed worked well, as long as there weren't a lot of waves. Seasickness was also a hazard, but you could at least take a nap until a rescue ship arrived. Say what you will, it was the world's first water bed!

A Foolish Fire Escape

The Parachute Hat

Go jump out the window! You could supposedly do it safely with the Parachute Hat. Its inventor called it "an improvement in fire escapes" when he patented it in 1879. In the event of a fire in a tall building, you could put on the hat, pull a cord, and soar to safety. A parachute would open on top of the hat and you would "land without injury and without the least damage." The maker also proposed an accessory to go with the Parachute Hat — a pair of shoes with thick shock-absorbing foam soles. If this wasn't the height of folly, it sure was close!

Just Horsing Around

Pony Preservers

How do you make a horse float? No — you don't take one horse and add soda and two scoops of ice cream. The answer is — or at least was in 1857 when this invention was patented — the Pony Preserver, a life jacket for horses. Keeping a horse's head above water while crossing wild rushing rivers is no joking matter. To make horses and their riders feel more at ease, this inventor devised two large inflatable floats that could be strapped to the horse's sides. The rider was supposed to blow up the floats using lung power alone. Once inflated, the Pony Preserver allowed horse and rider to float effortlessly across even the deepest stretch of water. The inventor failed to realize that horses can swim on their own, and that having two big balloons strapped to their flanks was more of a hindrance than a help. As a result, this invention was about as useful as screen doors on submarines.

Hands Across the Water

Combination Swimming Gloves and Life Preserver

Called "An Improvement in Swimming Gloves," this handy invention was supposed to be an aid to the recreational swimmer and a lifesaver in case of a shipwreck. The gloves floated, keeping the arms above water, or so the inventor said. But he was all wet, and so was this idea.

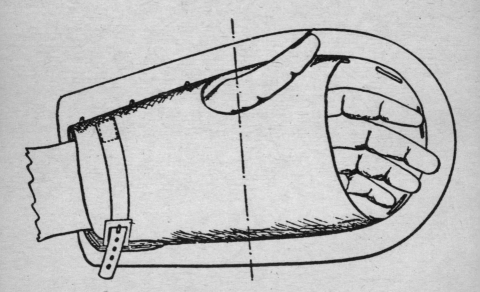

Wheel Things

"Stick to your $350-a-month job and stop tinkering with those automobiles," Henry Ford's father told him when the younger Ford made it known that he intended to go into the car-making business. Ford, of course, went on to invent a variety of cars that had a powerful impact on people's lives. The same can hardly be said for these wheeled wonders and travel aids.

Fight Without Flight

The Battlefield Bike

This would have made a great secret weapon for some army — it would have the enemy collapsing with laughter. The Military Bicycle, introduced at the outset of World War I, was an attempt to make bicycles suitable for the battlefield. Its inventor saw the bicycle as an inexpensive and quiet way to approach the enemy. Armored with a large bulletproof shield, it protected the rider's "lower extremities" from rifle fire. The inventor said the chest, arms, and head needed no such protection. "The upper part of the body," he said, "hanging low over the handlebars, does not offer an easy mark to hit when the rider is running swiftly on the bicycle." Noting that the shield was only in the front, the inventor pointed out that his bike was bulletproof, "unless you were running away from the enemy." It was best if the Military Bicycle were used only for one-way trips.

A Dog of an Idea

The Pet Perch

Everyone ought to travel in style, including the family dog. Or so believed the creator of the Pet Perch. When out for a drive, the family pooch was either forced to sit on the floor or annoy everyone by leaping across laps. The Pet Perch solved the problem. Now the family pooch had a place of its own. Not only did the Pet Perch keep Rover from roving, it also gave the pet what the inventor said was "a commanding view of the scenery." This doggie doodad may have been a hit with pets, but humans thought it was a real dog of an idea.

No Sale

The Sailomobile

Introduced in the 1920s, the Sailomobile was made out of homemade parts — fence pickets, old sheets, bike wheels, and ropes and pulleys. Powered by the wind, the Sailomobile looked like a sailboat on wheels. Steering was accomplished by turning a piece of wood connected to the front wheel. The inventor, an amateur hobbyist, admitted this was a lightweight idea, but he definitely didn't recommend that a lightweight use it. If that happened, the Sailomobile could become a flying machine and end up in a ditch along the side of the road. In the end, the Sailomobile went nowhere fast.

Racing Around the Grounds

The Bicycle Coffee Grinder

The Bicycle Coffee Grinder was a large coffee grinder attached to a bicycle. A chain connected the rear gear sprocket of the bike to a gear on the coffee grinder. The bike was set up off the ground, and as the rider pedaled in place, the grinder turned coffee beans into ground coffee. As the inventor pointed out, the bicycle provided an inexpensive way to grind coffee, and gave its owner a morning exercise session, too. But unless the rider was grinding coffee for the entire United States Army, the exercise session wouldn't last too long. In more ways than one, this invention was full of beans.

Wear It and Bear It

Windshields for One

In the 1920s, some cars didn't have windshields. Others had windshields that were too small or ineffective to provide much protection from wind and flying bugs. To give uneasy riders more protection, the inventor of this crazy car contraption suggested wearable windshields that hooked over the shoulders and rested on the chest. The idea didn't exactly drive people wild.

Down on the Farm

In the late 1800s and early 1900s, there was no bigger market for new products than the family farm. Many improvements in tools and farm machinery were made at this time. But farmers are famous for their good sense, which is why these homegrown inventions were never considered the cream of the crop.

A Fowl Idea

Eye Protector for Chickens

This birdbrained idea from 1902 was a real
eyeful, especially if you happened to be a chicken.
Farmers were often concerned about the damage
the birds could do to each other with their beaks.
So was this inventor. His Eye Protectors for Chickens looked like ordinary glasses. They rested on
the bird's beak and were held on by a wire around
the back of the head. Chicken farmers said this
fowl fashion was definitely not for the birds. They
didn't want their chickens making spectacles of
themselves.

You'd Get a Bang Out of It

The Plow Gun

You'd get a charge out of this farm tool. In 1862, when it was invented, the Wild West was pretty wild and a farmer had to have protection while plowing his fields. If attacked, the farmer could unhitch the horses and fire away at the enemy with a cannon built into the top of the plow. This may have made a boom, but it was really a bust.

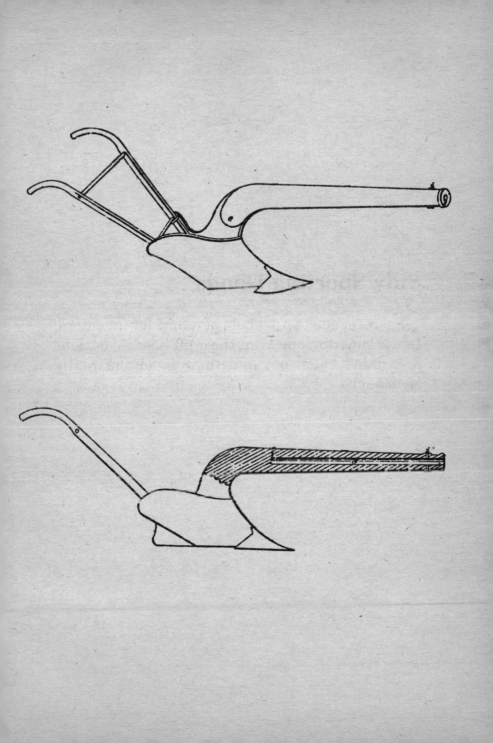

Silly Sporting Goods

Sports opened up a whole new field for inventors. In the long run, however, these off-base inventions just didn't catch on, and their inventors really struck out.

Too Much to Face

The Basketball Beauty Mask

This 1927 piece of sporting equipment was, in the inventor's words, "supposed to provide women basketball players with a means of protecting their faces and hair during strenuous games." Since it was only intended for women, one wonders whether the inventor believed that men players were too ugly to care about what happened to their faces, or too tough to care. The unlucky inventor found out that it was all over for his invention before the game had even begun. That's too bad, because it did offer a team one advantage. It was so ugly that the other side would probably be thrown off guard for the entire game.

A Booby Prize Catch

The Improved Fishhook

How dumb can fish be? In the opinion of the inventor of the 1894 Improved Fishhook, they are as dumb as they come. Fish would have to be stupid to swallow this fancy fishhook — a regular hook with a small mirror attached. The inventor believed that a fish would swim up to the mirror, mistake its reflection for a second fish, and try to get the bait first. It would "lose its caution and take the bait with a recklessness that increases the chances of being caught on the hook," the inventor said. For obvious reasons, fishermen just couldn't swallow this line of thinking.

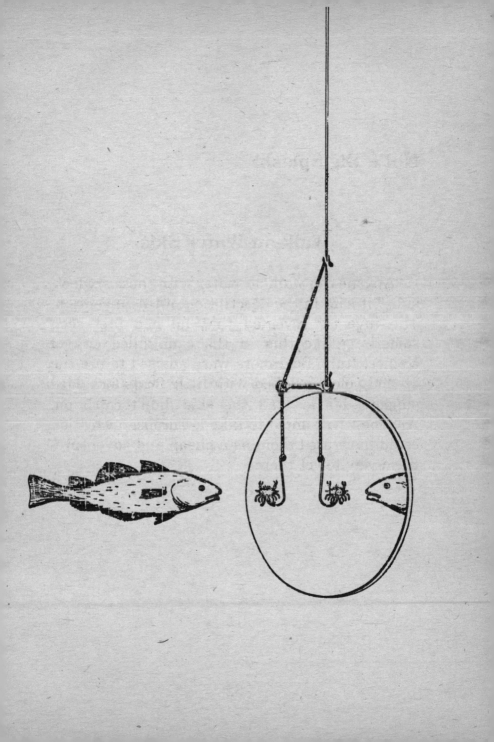

Not a Big Splash!

Walk-on-Water Skis

"Anyone can walk on water with these six-foot-skis," it said in the description of this invention. The inventor revealed that he had first seen something like this in the canal-filled city of Venice, Italy. Beginners were advised to use the special poles equipped with little floats for added support. It's too bad the skis didn't catch on. Anyone who wanted to take a European vacation could have used them as a cheap and adventure-filled way to get there.

Musical Madness

You didn't need a degree in music to master these instruments. Lessons were unnecessary and so was practice. With some, you didn't even need to use your hands to play them. Even so, these musical marvels never struck a responsive chord with aspiring musicians or the general public.

Look Ma, No Hands!

The Self-Playing Cornet

"The Self-Playing Cornet eliminates fingering," said a 1923 article about this English invention that resembled a player piano. A strip of paper with holes punched in it was fed into a device above the valves of the cornet. Mechanical fingers would do all the playing. You just had to blow into the mouthpiece. This instrument struck a sour note with musicians and everyone else.

The No Notes, Fold-up Practice Piano

How would you like to learn to play the piano without having to buy the large, expensive instrument? If that thought is music to your ears, this idea would be perfect for you. The 1909 Practice Piano had a full-sized keyboard of black and white keys — and nothing else. It was meant for beginners who had to practice tedious scales and finger exercises. Besides being economical, it had another advantage. It offered other members of the household fast relief from beginning piano students. As the inventor pointed out, "It never makes any nerve-wracking unmusical sounds." This was hardly surprising since it didn't make any sound at all!

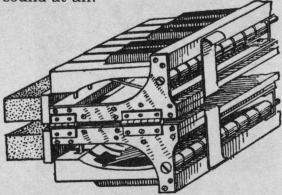

Noise to Go!

The Collapsible Cello

If the thought of a beginning piano student sends you climbing up the wall, just think about listening to a beginner trying to coax something musical out of a cello. A 1922 invention, the Collapsible Cello, took care of that problem. This French invention was collapsible and portable. The inventor, a young woman, claimed that "its skeleton body is so constructed that it is sufficiently mute to be heard only in the room where it is being played." Like the other musical marvels mentioned here, this invention collapsed and was never heard from again.

Miscellaneous Marvels

These cracked contraptions and mechanical marvels deserve to be in a class by themselves. That's because no one can quite figure out just where they belong, unless it's the local garbage dump.

May the Farce Be With You!

Movie Glasses

Lights! Camera! Action! That's what the movies are all about. According to some 1920s movie critics, the camera work and the action were fine, but the lights were a problem. It was thought that the bright light on the screen could damage moviegoers' eyes. To combat the glare, one movie-minded inventor created a special pair of glasses to be used while watching motion pictures. The glasses had dark opaque lenses that blocked all light except for what was admitted through a narrow slit in each lens. The glasses gave viewers the not-so-special effect of seeing a movie through what appeared to be a crack in a fence. For most people, movies don't cause eyestrain. These glasses, however, probably did.

A Crowning Achievement

Hats with Handles

During the 1920s, hats were considered an essential part of any stylish person's wardrobe. One of the most popular styles for women was a soft, brimless, tight-fitting hat that hugged the contours of the head. It was hard to pull off, however, and to solve this heady problem, one London hatter came up with what he thought was a hat-saving invention: a hat with handles sewn into the top. To remove the hat, all you had to do was pull the handle. This did not become the hatmaker's crowning achievement. A hat that looked like a suitcase was something well-dressed women could not handle.

A 1912 inventor believed that hats not only caused headaches, but also prevented people from showing off their hairstyles. His hat sat above the wearer's head, not touching the hair at all. The inventor said it was possible to turn your head without the hat moving. But this hat didn't turn any heads, and as a result vanished by 1913.

Heat to the Feet

Hot Air Footwarmer

Got cold feet? The pedal calorificator, or hot air footwarmer, could help. It was a series of tubes that were worn under the clothes and ended up at the feet. At the top was a mouthpiece that was held close to the mouth by a strap. By exhaling into the mouthpiece, hot air would be sent through the tubes down to the shoes, keeping the toes toasty. The inventor of this 1887 footwarmer suggested that it would be ideal for anyone traveling on an unheated train for several days. But the traveler did have to beware of one thing — inhaling! After all, that warm air had been circulating around the wearer's socks. This device could hardly be considered a breath of fresh air in the footwarmer field.

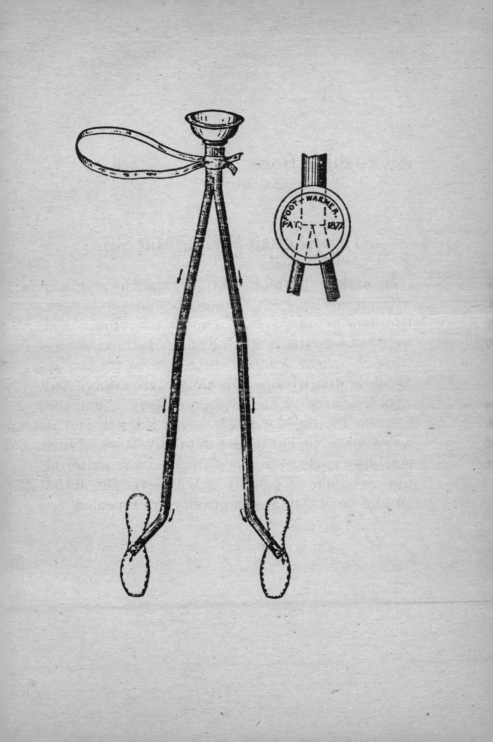

A Crashing Bore

The English Flying Machine

No book of oddball inventions would be complete without at least one ground-bound pre-Wright Brothers flying machine. One of the wildest and weirdest was the English Flying Machine, a contraption whose wings were supposed to flap up and down like a bird's. The wings were even coated with feathers! What could you say about the English Flying Machine? It was English and it was a machine, but it sure didn't fly. It was flying machines such as this one that led one writer of the era to joke, "These flyers will never get off the ground until the laws of gravity are repealed!"

Never Say Never!

Not all great inventions were welcomed when they first appeared on the scene. Which proves that some people just don't know a good thing when they see it, as you'll see.

"It takes too long to play. It is too complicated for children and the players have no final goal." — Parker Brothers Board of Directors, rejecting the game of Monopoly created by Charles Darrow in the early 1930s. They later changed their minds and sold over 80 million sets.

"Video will never be able to hold onto any market after the first six months." — Darryl F. Zanuck, a 20th Century-Fox movie studio boss, answering a question about the newly introduced television.

"Heavier-than-air flying machines are impossible." — Lord Kelvin, a prominent British scientist, commenting on the airplane in the 1890s.

"The present fad in locomotion is the automobile. It is a swell thing and the swell people must have one. But if it should displace the horse, it will only be for a short time." — The Louisville (KY) *Courier Journal,* 1900